THE GIFTS OF FORTUNE

Peter McDonald was born in Belfast in 1962.
His first book of poetry, *Biting the Wax*, was
published in 1989, and since then six volumes of
his verse have appeared, including his *Collected
Poems* (2012). He has written four books of
literary criticism, including *Mistaken Identities:
Poetry and Northern Ireland* (1997) and *Sound
Intentions: The Workings of Rhyme in Nineteenth-
Century Poetry* (2012). He is Professor of
British and Irish Poetry in Oxford University.

Also by Peter McDonald

Herne the Hunter
The Homeric Hymns
Collected Poems
Torchlight
The House of Clay
Pastorals

PETER McDONALD

The Gifts
of Fortune

CARCANET

First published in Great Britain in 2020 by
Carcanet
Alliance House, 30 Cross Street
Manchester M2 7AQ
www.carcanet.co.uk

A CIP catalogue record for this book is
available from the British Library.
ISBN 978 1 78410 943 1

Book design by Andrew Latimer
Printed in Great Britain by SRP Ltd, Exeter, Devon

MIX
Paper from
responsible sources
FSC
www.fsc.org   FSC® C014540

The publisher acknowledges financial
assistance from Arts Council England.

Supported using public funding by
ARTS COUNCIL
ENGLAND

Contents

THE GIFTS OF FORTUNE

alle ben yiftes of fortune,
That passen as a shadwe upon a wal.

■

Shadows – hold their Breath –

■

WEAVELEY FURZE (1)

for G.H.

So: to keep going on the glum route-march,
a mile's trudge in the summer across fields
where either a dropped match
or the farmer on purpose burned the crop
crisp black; or else sunshine, that nothing shields
us from; or else dumb mischief; till we stop
at a thin gate with a rope latch
fraying from the top.

The Glyme and the Dorn, not even half full
are not so much as half heard, yet the trees
make their leaves voluble
as they wobble like water overhead.
Down here, sticky brambles with homebound bees
inheriting their commonwealths, instead
of this binding, unenforceable
contract with the dead

that no one can believe in any more,
spread at their own speeds; now at your deaf side
I lessen the uproar
but can't pretend the noise has gone away.
Someone has cut logs into sticks, and tied
them in faggots, and left them: you could say
they're sound, or rotten at the core,
mugging pure dismay:

ghastly, ghastly. Maybe it's just the heat,
or the staginess of advancing years,
but the young do seem to bleat
(I'm younger; I'm not young) a deadly din
round and about us now while, *unawares,*
something expires. Still there's nothing to win:
the courage, just, to leave your seat,
take breath, and begin.

2015

THE DROVERS' ROAD

wonders that have happened
On wet roads where men walk

Bad weather for a fortnight now.
I scramble uphill in mud
over the steep field, as below
me among trees the Glyme floods,

catching daylight and trapping it
far down from here, down and away,
while my feet slide and slip out
of step – too long, then suddenly

too short a stride, and all
the effort not to fall, but just
keep upright, keep moving, until
one way or another I get past

the ground where it turns to river
and put the shoes I stand up in
back on the drovers' road. There
ought to be ghosts: the put-upon,

labouring every day for ever
and poor in death even, who go
ahead with all their lives lived
out once on the terms given,

cold, in boots that are letting in,
up and down the muddy road
that they don't know how to leave,
and mightn't leave, if they could.

My own people were labourers;
beside them, I'm a rich man; I
stumble my way along the verge
and nobody beckons me across.

There's nothing from them as they trudge
away from here and back, many
with less than they brought, and many
with not even that much.

Flashes of daylight on a screen-glance of sun;
the ambient new smell, and silence well paid for
as a body snoozes its untold planet-time
in the middle of things, costly things everywhere,
bespoke, agleam, the things instead of love;
not to last, like prayers that are vain: *Let
the work of my hands be broken. Let the doors
stand open and the cold come in.*

CINEMATIC

Too late, but not too late for me to hide
these sorry features further in the shade,
as huge projected faces loom and slide

away into their screen; I want to go
where images and ghosts stagger and slow,
past time that passes over or below

my heart shunting its blood too late; and as
the screenlight glances from her now, she is
beautiful like a star in the silent pictures,

all eyes, all eyes, and twice her lifesize tall,
falling away from me, into nightfall.
A shadow leaves its shadow on the wall.

AVENTINE

In a garden beneath dusty orange trees
the little sparrows are three-quarters dust
as they loiter near, then dance away from these
teenagers kissing as if this was the last

evening on earth – I don't know where to look,
still less to pick up just where I left off
in the other century; but I've kept safe
all the way up, in a bag slung on my back,

two glasses, here, and this chilled bottle.
I pour it, we drink, and stare straight ahead:
I know your eyes so well that I daren't look
when I say I've come straight from a funeral

and here we are, somehow; somehow I'm back
at six in the evening, in Rome instead,
raising a glass with you. And then I turn,
as our wine lights up like the sunset-burn

over an ashy path I climb and climb,
and see your face: we're not at the right time,
or any time, but our hands touch. When we kiss,
shyly at first, nobody notices.

AT THE END OF THE WORLD

Why it should be Portballintrae, I don't know, yet
here we all are, sharing this last afternoon,
hundreds of us; maybe no one has stayed inland.
As I lean on a railing with a good view up the coast
it strikes me as odd that everything doesn't happen at once,
time rolled up, and all that: but clearly it's going
to be gradual, an outdoor movie, starting
with this big-scale light-show, the sky a single
baby-blue all the way up, and then the sun
fixing itself in an unsophisticated yellow
to the one spot; as though it had thought better
than to make a fuss, the sea has no waves, and if
you look long enough, has become transparent;
no boats out there, I notice, though behind me cars
are still arriving, people parking where they like
and coming to watch. Nothing has actually happened
as yet, and it's hard to stay in the right mood, with dogs
sniffing each other up, and the children getting bored,
while just to one side of me a gaggle of the saved
have run out of things to pray, and are singing instead.
Did they expect this exactly? Probably not,
though a few, I see, have thought to bring sandwiches:
I wonder if my Aunt Lizzie is even now at work
in heaven, preparing welcome plate after plate of
sausage rolls, shortbread, big sponges and traybakes?
I hope so. Nobody is managing very much
in the way of conversation, and I suppose we are all
trying to concentrate, in our own ways, though that

can't go on forever. The sun now is the sun
in a painting; the breeze drops, picks up again,
drops; I'm looking at my watch for some reason,
then back at the view, which hasn't really changed, and
is starting to seem a little bit bland: I'd have liked
something more vivid, Blakean, but everybody seems
happy enough. I think they're still selling ice-cream.

LESSONS

The tedium
of other people's dreams
is nothing to the tedium
of your own:
maybe in a lifetime

a handful tell
the kind of truth you somehow
needed to have known.
Two that still rattle
in my skull

both come from
(I think) my twentieth year.
In the first one, I meet
a fully-armoured man,
and freeze with fear

in the ancient
bottleneck of Catte Street,
having nowhere to run
when he strikes hard down:
his horse is white

and the crest
on his helmet is green.
Then, in the other one,
I am back at home
where the worst

of bad weather
drives lines of wind and rain
up from Donegall Pass
to where I am, between
Bradbury Place

and the Lisburn Road,
lying on my own arm
but with my legs splayed
across gutter and kerb:
the shots came

from the head
of Sandy Row, but it's all
quiet, and the quieter
now for my faceful
of dirty water,

dirtier
with blood; but then disturbed
by a hard voice in arrears,
its quick contempt
– *mickdanalt!* –

and that's it,
no meaning and no message,
for my eyes can't engage;
I feel nothing: my ears
fill up with silt.

ANATOMY

Someone tell the boy:
let him know, before
time can close the door
on bright hearts, on joy,

all that's not to fear;
nothing in the night
ever touches quite
what is safest here.

Let him keep it safe
while the body grows
into all it knows:
years that bruise and chafe,

months that weigh it down
with such heavy strength,
tender-tough at length,
and the tears that drown

days and weeks, like some
cloud too big to see
coming, or to be
dodged when it does come.

Tell him all the truth
far beneath the skin:
death and life begin
there together, youth

keeps inside it age,
and the memory
needs what it can't see
while these muscles rage

in, then out of, life;
ecstasy that serves
terror to the nerves
like a pin-thin knife

drilled-in with blood-rain,
and then flesh degloved
for the women loved
once, and not again.

MYSTERY

The trippers' buses would be parked up outside
Barry's Amusements, and I passed them every day
as my orbit narrowed beyond where they stood
idle, first closer then right into the play
of lighting and bells,

sparky dodgems, all the rubber- and oil-smells
from the rides, a jabber and clunk of bright machines,
and jangles of copper coins, falling at intervals
like cataracts of money that sluiced unseen
in echoey space,

where I'd move each time at a newcomer's pace,
cautious and curious and utterly absorbed.
The long buses outside were dozing in place,
with their destination blackboards undisturbed –
Derry and Coleraine,

exotic Donegal: sealed up, empty and hot,
they were all waiting for their rides to begin,
like the one just called *Mystery*: where would it not
go, I wondered, and could it even be seen
skirting the sea-bay

away up the coast, and giving nothing away,
full of shadows who don't speak? A spaceship
might thunder-rumble overhead, and then dip;
if I left, I'd just return as a boy
riding the ghost-train.

SUCCESS
Pindar

Two things only, two things above all
make your life perfect and delightful
in the blossom and blossoming over
of pure wealth: first the doing well,
success; and then later when you hear
from everyone
how well it is you've done.

No need to try for more – why bother
to pass for God when what you have is
all that there is
if even a little is your share?
We all know riches
pass away; and we pass away too,
alone, with our mortal goods in tow.

AMBITION

High up, the luxuries include
silence, a quality of air
all hush and light and no dust,
not so much as an inch of shade

where things work by being at rest,
and it all costs: riches are sad,
but to go high, even higher
than this, you must see past the good,

and none of it is just for show:
you can stare right down into sorrow
like a gaping well where water
pours for ever into the ground:

this is all of all you wanted
(the truth is, you have forgotten
whatever you wanted then),
so eye-bound and light-headed,

so high up over everything
but with no floor, with no ceiling,
that nobody could ever fall
from looking in the deep-drawn well.

CAREER

Tempers must have been lost on all sides – my fault –
when McClartey gave my parents his assessment
of what the future held: *a hewer of wood, and
a drawer of water* (knowing that the Biblical
would cut deep) and then, in case more was needed,
he'll end up sweeping the streets. From then on
they would receive letters addressed to 'The Braniel
Housing Estate' just to make the point, to drive
it into the home, where every night I'd still
go to sleep in fear of a fist-hammered window,
ten years of age and desperate to escape
when the only way out was to get over the exam,
though I still forgot what was beaten into me,
and the harder I tried the more I forgot,
night-angers crashing and splintering in my head,
and my head a mess; but everything was falling
down and apart, explosions were like the weather,
and nobody slept, for everyone was on edge –
McClartey with the cane down his trouser pocket,
thuggish Pinnerton, beating a child every day,
or Mr Potter, talking deliriously about Jesus
and how the end of the world was coming any time now:
nobody was quite sane, anywhere you looked.

Years later, every Christmas at charity
collection-time, when McClartey used to rattle
the tin on Royal Avenue, my father would
go looking for him, to ask if maybe he'd seen
Peter sweeping the streets lately, or cleaning
the mud-choked gutters in Belfast? As far
as I know, he never found him: they're both dead now,

and the truth is, I skivvy and clear away mess
after the poets, invisible beside them,
their hewer of wood and their drawer of water
if only on my better days, days when I see
the thing that might be missed, pick it up, and
leave it where someone will know to look, keeping
well out of sight, and making sure that nobody
knows me, or knows where it is I go home to.

CONUNDRA

for A. W. O.

           I remember
           being sixteen
    less well than you remember
    being sixteen, but there
           is the single-bar
           electric fire
    that was still glowing then
           into the colder air
of my bedroom through the early hours
    in that terraced house of ours,
as next door shouted half the night,
           every so often
           slamming some weight
with big drunk screams, *Fuck UP, all right?*
    always the woman's voice,
           Fuck UP, you fuck UP!
I would be balancing my cup
between the desk and dark, one sip
           from making the choice
           in a painful case
           where God and time
and no-time and no-God were face
    to face and hand to hand
across a void, or not a void;
           where Dante's Paradise
           with its vast rose
bellowed across a black, unscanned
gap that I still couldn't avoid;
    and all that the heart knows

today is less
than the sleepless fear
and jitter-nerved sheer
attention then,
starting to focus
on the little piece
of something that had landed on
those orange wires wrapping the bar
like a jap of tar,
dark, smoking, with a fringe of white
spreading where that minute
blip of combustion
became a burnt-on flaw;
I told myself that what I saw
was the finite
marking the face of infinity,
but I couldn't fix
Belfast metaphysics –
fuck UP, fuck UP – I couldn't see
any path to take me
from an equation
that wouldn't come out anyway;
and the small hours rolled away,
puzzling into day
as I walked off with a swelled head
up Dunluce Avenue,
its straight line going on and on
like a line to toe or tread
between the beautiful and the true,
or just a line
without design

or purpose, something all unmeant
                         that came and went
while I was labouring to be
in a pattern I would never see:
Platonic line – *fuck UP, fuck UP* – ,
the Lisburn Road, and the bus stop.

CASHLESS

Look at me, keep looking, and see me, please,
not as I am but as I am flooded

by something more than just the light; see me
walking beneath a tree-ceiling of banknotes:

the notes are leaves; I am hooded in green leaves
and happiness, pacing away to nowhere

on a crooked mud-road, fresh now from its nights
of penury, a sunburst of lit jade

where living trees are spirits of the dead
that shed money, waiting for me to pass.

And if you look at me, don't see me here;
there's nothing I won't give to touch your hand,

to put it into my hand made from leaves
like the ghosts of riches: I will pay for this.

DOUBLE NAME

A whole sky ready to be dark;
now the last of the day is going
out into blue light, a light-mark,
and by it a half-moon, showing

the way to somebody now – not me,
but maybe you, for all I can tell,
who set a course by the star you see
while that blue covers you as well:

just the one sky for everyone,
where even different names are right
depending on what's seen or done,
and us at either edge of the night

not meeting, our own names unsaid,
me out at dawn with you everywhere
in my head, and there overhead
a half-moon, and the morning star.

A PROSPECT

So much, you couldn't ask for more; but more
comes, and you take it: plenteous with summer,

elms cushion an extravagant sky; all
needs that could be created, catered for:

even when you want it to hurt, even then
in the soft light, enough won't register –

intricate puppet shadows, and no sign
of the far side of everything you have.

SILENT

They talk and talk; but her two eyes
    take all the words away
into some future half the size
    of what a voice can say,

a future made out of the past,
    jagged and fragile bits
of lines belonging to the cast
    of a film where nothing fits

their moving mouths, because the sound
    was never even there;
a silent picture someone found
    in its rusting tin of air:

and her eyes are the living eyes
    of a mute movie-star
returning from the past that dies
    to where his questions are,

those questions that he asks in vain
    and she must never hear,
for it's too early to explain
    how love's in sync with fear,

and how those eyes tell everything
    he wants, how he can't wait
for long ago, for time to bring
    her now, while it's too late.

CRAB-APPLES

You aren't here with me, and it doesn't matter.
I have been walking with you half the night,
and either I have been sleeping upright
or this is no dream the dawn can shatter:

mud under our boots, slippery black leaves,
fallen crab-apples that are rotting down;
over our heads bare branches and a crown
of sky where one tiny bird skits and weaves.

We are talking, talking; we are holding hands,
and it's as though there's no time left to save;
I think we might be visiting my grave
somewhere along this way, where the bird lands

and crab-apples are fermenting underfoot
so that the air is tart with them, until
there's no more space for that air to fill
and everything stays where it's been put.

There are no shadows: there are only light
and dark in solid forms, not moving;
there is nothing that needs testing or proving
any more, there is nothing out of sight:

I am a young man and in love with you
for ever still, whose head swims, and I am
an old man heavy with remorse and shame
facing back on all this, to face it through.

MYTH

I meet her every ten years or so –
the joy is less joy than sorrow,

but it's still what she leaves me with,
every last dream of her a myth:

always she's standing under trees
in leaf-light, her eyes mysteries

that start with love, but go somewhere
remote, cold as the coldest air

and as invisible; I may
be too weak finally to say

the word, that word, she came to give:
nobody can say it and live.

AT NEWCASTLE ISLAND

for Alan and Philippa

Should the sunshine on Kanaka Bay
ever bring itself to give way

to cloud or shadows or dark night,
when purple martins in their flight

are buoyant for eternity
over a cold and flashing sea?

THE SEALS

We'd laugh, wouldn't we,
telling each other the story
of how he sat out
all that morning by the sea

between Downhill and Portstewart
(on a bench, admittedly),
convinced that he'd spotted
seals at play

near the grey-and-white
churn of Atlantic water;
how he came back later,
chuckling as he reported

nothing but rocks and waves?
The one day when I did
get clear sight of a seal,
there was no one to tell:

I'd left you, I believe,
in the ward, and had taken
one of those short drives
that end at the coast

(the fact is, they'll all
end up there). I saw most
of the way to Ballylumford;
it was only the Lough,

but even so, there and then,
I was looking at a seal
just yards off, a seal
that was taking its sweet time

with nothing to do:
and I stopped too,
for in that instant I knew
I had met him again,

and each back-bob and head-turn
meant he had come to wait
for you; he was good at waiting.
But he said No, not now,

and saw me to the light
of the shore when I turned to go
back to our used-up lives;
warm-blooded, patient for you,

a seal keeping watch till
you'd come, another seal
in the cold water with nothing
but rocks and waves.

TO FALL INTO THE HANDS

A sky that could deliver either thunder or snow
– orange-grey, virulent, and lit from the one side –
takes up two thirds of the picture, where that shadow
is me, and yet still somehow no, isn't mine;
and if I claim I'm afraid, remember that fear is
cheap: the phone ringing, wind slamming a door shut,
or the stranger meeting your glance with a hard stare.
Cheap things barely register: ten-a-penny
daydreams that start with me holding her hand in
mine, just holding her hand, but end badly
in torn letters, anger, pillows full of tears,
the fear of meeting, or meeting my face in the mirror
where it shows all it has done – look at it, look:
every sag and wrinkle and blotch is a judgement,
as well as a sure sign of the judgement to come.

Shadows are better: that shadow under the sky
may yet speak, but will it be afraid, afraid
enough of the hands that can touch it and hold it,
hold it for ever or else allow it to fall
deep away, out into clouds built of light
but bundling smoke in dull, sun-cancelling
billows that trail into red and dust-soiled pink?

Like a bad taste, an obscure sense rises
that money's no help, no end of money,
and this is a reckoning: reckon with this,
with time and fatigue, death weighing your face down
as it weighs you up and takes your full measure.
Even in those hands, you're still thinking, aren't you,
of her hands and the single day they held yours,

her pulse you could feel connecting with your own
as if suddenly you were twice alive and more
than life-size, oh as if she could hear you
speak to yourself while you tried to bear up the sky,
knowing the whole time what can't be admitted,
that the audience is really an audience of one,
that the clouds are just weather, that everything's
true and too late, that this is the fearful thing?

MUD

voices of prophecy assail the dead

I.

There were books in the downstairs toilet
– the downstairs loo, he'd have called it –
with *Observer Magazine*s, and *Listener*s,
a Penguin *Gawain*, selected Eliot,
that year's Booker, some others
falling over themselves to fit in:
the new Hughes; Tony Harrison.

I brought the last one out with me,
to drink (of all things) dry sherry
at two o'clock in the afternoon
in St. John's Wood, but Bloomsbury
was all around us. We moved on
to Yeats: *He addressed me, 'Young man,'*
turning that monocle my way,

'what are your views on the Sayers?'
I was terrified: I thought he meant
some group of lady verse-performers
from County Galway, so I went
vague and said I hadn't heard them,
unfortunately: all the time
he was thinking of a whodunit!

I laughed in the right accent: that was
the poet who, he'd announced once,
wrote by saving himself from the mud
of Flanders: much was understood
without being said, then and since.
I asked him for some instances
of poetry he liked nowadays:

I do think Hill's a bit of a fraud –
Wystan asked me about his book,
the first one: 'Stephen, it's no good,
is it?' And I said No, it's not.
But Harrison now, (he'd taken a look
at what I was holding in my hand)
Harrison I like a tremendous lot;

I feel that all my life I've been
waiting for him to come along.
I was making sure to understand,
stuck in *the mud of the common mind*
(a phrase he didn't remember writing)
and young enough to want to belong
here among all he'd heard and seen.

The talk was turning to MacNeice:
Louis was wonderful, but the rot
set in once he would only see
that drinking set from the BBC,
all boors, and awful Irishmen.
I agreed, trying to look wise
in hindsight: I'd hardly begun.

2.

The stiff earth, and furrows of dusty clay
      all winter take their way
back towards liquid, where I step slipshod
      in sump after sump of mud

almost wanting it now to suck me down,
      unstoppable, sudden
like extra gravity, into the kind of dark
      where I, like all my work,

will be mixed slowly, indistinguishably
      with dirt, and whatever we
deserve, in an element whose clutches
      soil all that it touches:

for my voice is hard with grit, and thick with muck,
      words gurgling far back
as angry noises, undrownable, chock-full
      of themselves, implacable.

3.

The background that a mirror shows
   looks real, and it could be:
these red-brick houses cramped in rows
   that run miles behind me

are streets in Ballyhackamore
   where my grandmother lives
with her husband before the War;
   hundreds of other wives

and husbands pack the houses there;
   even the curate, John
MacNeice (he's not their minister),
   who has as yet not gone

onwards and upwards, with his family
   still growing – the Mongol boy,
a little girl, and a baby, Freddy.
   The big houses employ

her to skivvy in Castlereagh:
   on her hands and knees she does
the flags in Strandtown – in Little Lea,
   look, for the Lewises –

and only housemaids know her name;
   she is Sarah, or Mrs. Moore:
in that job she has to become
   nothing, scrubbing the floor

with a pail of dirty water. A few
     years on, her man comes back
from Gallipoli, but he's too
     far away with the shock

to know her; he goes off again
     to France, and the winter mud
that sucks him in and takes him down
     as she dreaded it would.

She sees him sometimes, covered head
     to foot in blood and muck;
he wipes soil from his lips, instead
     of saying he'll come back.

4.

I know what he meant – Dodds, that is,
when people pressed him to give his
real opinion of this place:
I hate it, he would say, *It's full
of* clever *people*: that wise face
was his way of keeping counsel –
one gift that I'll never possess.

My features must give me away:
flabby and soft-drawn, glum with age,
there's nothing here that you could say
adds up to character; instead,
the components of a clown-head
stare and gape up from a page
at the assembled committee –

they have my measure. Denniston
was supposed to have been given the job,
or else Bowra, that facile snob,
but it went to Dodds, decided on
by none other than Stanley Baldwin,
with whom Murray had had a word
– Gilbert Murray, whom they abhorred,

and didn't speak to for twenty years,
all those dead men with names that mean
nothing, just gossip for deaf ears
that almost nobody understands.
The clever people stare me down
again here, all these decades on;
there's a sudden lavish wave of hands

as one with the bray of authority
pronounces *The House mustn't be
dragged down into the Irish mud*,
and his disgusted glance towards me
explains that better than he could.
Arguments are too long and sore
for me to argue any more.

Dodds walks me back across Tom Quad.
In the War, he was an orderly
on a hospital ship: months at sea
with puke and shit and blood, and God
knows what ankle-deep on the floors;
boys dying in the corridors
would choke and ramble, cough and cry.

Childless, his pair of almost sons
had died on him – Louis, Wystan –
but as far as this place… His wise head
shakes slowly. Now he hears how I
was asked once whether Yeats was *mad,
a bit* Irish, *yes?* The reply
is far off, and leaves me alone.

5.

The softer the clay, the gloopier, the more
    it can absorb, and the more force
gets lost in it; as huge shells in the War
    dropped and erupted and made worse

those spreading lagoons of mud. Natural
    shocks – *Yes, yes*, Geoffrey would say,
not an inheritance but a requital
    for the flesh – have to make their way

into self-portraits, where the very worst thing
    looks back at you, stupid and soiled,
craving the love that you must never bring
    it, there to be mocked and assailed:

the true self-portrait is an ugly one,
    it takes strength and it soaks up strength;
mirrors can only show you what has gone
    while you posed for them at full length.

You came from nothing: you are only made
    from clabber, made from mire and blood,
so back you go, too thick to be afraid,
    dragging your own name through the mud.

CLUB BAR

You were still far from being born,
but I was closer than I knew
        to never coming through
        my teens unmaimed, untorn,
to never seeing what I'd sworn
to see, to never leaving home
and risking what I might become
in time, to never meeting you;
        that evening when I swam
through early summer light and air
        down Dunluce Avenue,
        my head a record-player
(it was *Astral Weeks* then, and *Blood
        on the Tracks*, both borrowed
        by the week from Dougie Knight's),
lightening and lighting up there
my route down College Gardens, and then on
        up University Road
until the arranged destination
        floated into my sights:
        the Club that night, the Club Bar,
selected to be not too far
        for anyone, that showed
a plain face, with its locking grille,
to the world; and past those iron gates
a lounge with nothing unusual,
the one big table with us all
        around it, neatly stowed
lifting underage pints like weights
in a dark corner, not to be seen;
smoke and banter, glasses half-full.

As I broke a struck match
between two fingers, everything
                stopped, and a wrong
                sound, solid as the wall,
lifted and covered us: stock-still,
                I was able to watch
                every bottle explode
behind the bar, and pieces fly
                slowly in millions by
                through sheets of drink, and when
                real time started again
I was drenched in booze, with bits of glass
                like little shreds of ice,
                and not so much as a scratch
on me; my wet, exposed, white skin
                untouched while the whole place
in darkness emptied into the dark,
                and we shuffled past police
arriving, to a road berserk
                with horns and flashing lights.
                I walked out with my life
                in my hands, and carrying
the gifts of fortune, everything
                good as new, and as safe,
not knowing where to go: I got
                as far as a sheltered spot
above Mount Charles (Mount Charles, where I
was born), and I sat down to dry
                out, or just sat to wait
since there was nothing else to do,
for other nights, and years, and you.

SOOTH

What he didn't know (he was
still a boy) was that it
turns out there *is* a limit
to what you can imagine,

but when he crunched the bones
underfoot he had no cause
to think so. Waiting beside
the sooth voice of the shade

– a few steps of cracked stone –
I get stuck now on
sooth, like a false note
snagging the melody's run:

sooth, sooth – but he was young;
he would be gone soon,
and he liked the sound. (I am
so far from being born

that I can imagine him
only by faking it,
for the country of youth
is a far planet where

you can't even breathe.)
It has nothing to do
with *soothe*, it means *true*;
and there's too much of that,

truth, on the other side
of everything you have:
for all he saw or said,
there was no need to believe

what was so plain, a stab
and not a sound, a crinkle
in the light, unstable
words on their white slab,

and he was thankful
maybe, soothed, never to
feel that; just to call
it misery and have done.

Eventually, you can't bear
to see, can't bear to feel
what you couldn't stall;
you have your limits

though he never found his,
a given, no more,
at the bruised horizon;
and it is what it was,

what the reflexes knew:
something about no end
of real things, sore and
meaningless in the sun.

MUSE

All night, I see her watching eyes
in the dark where I am out of place,

and where they have no cause to be;
now, I think, they must find the lies

that spread across my beaten face.
She goes away so gradually

it takes an age for me to notice
those eyes are Indian, and further

away than any sight could bear:
they are too truthful and too wise

to stay where they are out of place
in darkness for my watching eyes.

THE OTHER SIDE
Filippino Lippi

She holds a dress that holds
itself around her, moves
between its forms and folds
in a slow dance that proves

the stillness kept away
from all that's at first sight:
such secrets in display
are love's secrets, and right

behind the sad half-man,
she smiles through a sweet song
we can't hear, and she can,
as though nothing was wrong.

Behind her silence, sound;
behind the man a boy;
behind the scar a wound;
behind the wound the joy.

UNPACKING THE MICHELANGELO

On its wheels, the crate is a good
three or four inches off the ground
– useful for the half-hour it stood
in a tarmac puddle at JFK
waiting for papers to be found –
an oblong box made of new wood
still splintery around the sides,
stickered and barcoded the way
anything might be; now it glides
with the gentlest push along the floor
of the storeroom up to a table
we've cleared for it, a surface where
cutters and pliers and wire cable
have good room to accumulate:
it takes two of us to lift it
and lay the case completely flat.

Screwdrivers first: an ordinary
counter-clockwise turn of the wrist
is enough to loosen every
one of the dozen threaded pins
that held an outside panel fast,
which then will simply lift away
to lean lightly against a wall
while the peeling open begins,
and layers of thick coating fall
down to the ground; stiff fasteners
come out, and plastic brackets snap,
shock-swallowing foam finally stirs
and bounces from the bubble-wrap

covering an exhibition frame
beneath whose glass the very same
drawing is back now whence it came.

I hold it up into the light,
and black chalk from five centuries
ago is still fresh as first sight
while I bring it close up, a page
with tiny writing no one sees
and only I now can set right.
Thousands have looked this closely though,
and nothing here that I can gauge
will count for much, as these things go;
it weighs so little, and yet all
it's been worth, and it will be worth,
is past counting, elemental
like tons of gold deep in the earth:
but in my two hands, at least where
rain keeps washing the window clear,
it waits for me to disappear.

IN BILLIONS

Here is an image of her hand – the hired hand –
into which they have slipped a glass of *Kristal*
on their private jet bound for the Carribean,
while they turn up the music, getting steadily drunker,
and she takes care of the Brat, who says nothing
and hates them: out in the sky there are billions
of atoms free to dart around in the atmosphere
that nobody has bought – look, you can't see them –
where they make as much sense as invisible money
while a tube of wealth shoots through them and away,
only to go where it has to come back from.

I think of her breathing in the recycled air
as if she might breathe in gold, or some purer
cold alchemical light that fills up the plane,
the spirit of riches, spirit of altitude;
I imagine slipping my hand into hers, and
taking from it gently that warming champagne
to put there instead a glass of something better
that tastes of earth and raindrops and the bare sun,
of time and sadness, but sadness going away,
all depth and finish, not one tenth of the price,
for her to tilt into that vanishing morning.

THE PARTY
Horace

What we have here is a case of nine-
    year-old Chassagne
Montrachet, chilled and ready to go;
    the thing to do

next, darling, is to take your pick
    of aromatic
micro-herbs from the garden, grown
    to be jade-green,

and set them as a final touch
    of colour to catch
the eye in your styled and piled-up hair,
    so everything here

flashes with star-light straight from you:
    now the whole show
gets ready, as everyone obeys
    orders, the boys

and girls on the staff bustle all
    around, a cowl
of smoke hangs over the new-lit
    flambeaux, that shoot

across mirrors of set-out silver
    by the stall where
lamb steaks wait for the barbecue
    in one long row.

You should know why you've been invited
    to a party started
this day in April every year,
    held in honour

not of my birthday (I don't care
    at all), but for
my dear friend's, since he likes to see
    his life click by;

and now that you are here don't, please,
    get any ideas
about having a second chance
    with the young man

another woman has taken by storm –
    she's on his arm
for ever, and he won't want you
    again – so now

remember how high horses throw
    even rodeo-
riders, and fine-tune your sights
    back to what suits

you best, when what you settle for
    is best by far,
all things considered. Come with me
    in the brightly

glittering dark, and be the last
    girl on the list
of a few women that I loved
    in the time I lived;

learn the proper words to the song,
   and start to sing
so grief, that tracks us all the way,
   is kept at bay.

THE ROOMS

No ghost bothers to haunt the rooms
   where sunlight comes and goes;
tree-peonies' great wasted blooms
   from outside seem to pose

at the window, pleading there in rags
   like spoiled grave-finery,
begging against some weight that drags
   them to their last decay.

And insects fill the air outside;
   outside belongs to them,
the sun is where they go to hide,
   a fulgent stratagem

ungraspable in this trapped air
   breathed in and out all day,
the room a box that's been snapped shut,
   their world anything but –

like abstract nouns, or easy rhymes
   all too easy sometimes:
immortality, infinity,
   start to sicken and die

in the blind room that senses far
   away a closing muse
whose name is death, whose agents are
   the bee and the butterfly.

GUINEA

The Eye sees more than the Heart knows.

That flat disk is a star, but here
it moves, as it goes into clouds
then out of them, steady white fire
somewhere above and behind the air
it fills, air that it loads

indifferently, at no cost,
for you to see things in – though what
you see depends, and you're the last
to know what it depends on, lost,
exhausted, dead in the heart,

beneath a disk of fire: it is pure
as money, as gold, the vast day
that empties you and leaves you poor,
its pitch of vision pitched too far,
deep-lighted, flaming away.

GILNAHIRK ROAD

A whole month's rainfall in one day:
I remember when I could fly
weightless up this hill, all the way

to where I stand now, heavy, wet,
with breath gone in the air, and not
able to budge from where I've set

my two feet in the grass and loam,
while strict rain lashes me like time
that eats away the marks of home,

and whittles everything I have
down to this age, sopping the twelve
white roses I brought for their grave.

CROSSING THE LINE

They went away one by one
over the fear and pain,
and that was the last of them:
now I am all alone

I can think of them together
and say that I see them, out
walking the horizon,
having slipped a barrier

I can't see, and can't cross,
while grief cries tears of shame
and still is at a loss
to say why, or to look

into the light where they move –
light of sunset, light of
the evening star –
when nothing could be more

bare than this; but they've gone
even beyond the line
I crossed by being born;
gone one by one, alone.

FINITY

Small blocks of painted wood: the cubes were blue,
a dark blue that was grey-blue now with age;
some days at Gilnahirk in Primary Two
I used to stack as many as I could manage,

then squint down from the top, down the blue edge
of storey upon storey nearly in line,
till I was balancing along a ledge
one made over another: eight or nine

was higher than the highest thing on earth,
and that made me unmeasurably tall
as I took breath, and jumped for what I was worth
further than anyone could ever fall.

A lifetime later, and the trees in line
on a summer road are slim green cylinders
all the same height, standing here by design
to look from the ground like an unending series

that I pass slowly. In my bones there are years,
but the distance I cover is real – here is
the next turn in the road, here is the next –
and I'm liable to think on, without pretext,

long past myself, on some other long walk
in the city, beside thin rectangles of road,
the day I walked away out to Finaghy;
now there are places I would wait to talk

to them, this one or that one I might see
on the way, though I know well enough the dead
are really just people who have stopped
when the same things happen on and on ahead.

As though there was much to say, when there's not:
the flat, thick, yellow circles, moved and gone;
a red wooden pyramid, then another one.
Sure I'll be all right here; away you on.

BLINDNESS

□

■

Your blindness wasn't blindness but
confusion between sharp and blurred,
the centres of everything cut
out and to pieces, then scattered
along each edge. You couldn't see,
which meant really that what you saw
never cohered again: see me,
empty, a gap of fleck and flaw,
where nothing's stable or in place.
Look straight through the hole in my face.

■

Once light starts to go wrong, the whole
world shrinks, becomes cramped and held back:
or you hold back, scared of it all,
testing spaces with a white stick,
your arm over mine as you stare
hard at the ground that vanishes
by steps, until the nothing there
rises to meet you, finishes
up here, with barely room to turn
around: I look, and never learn.

■

The time you would have walked this road
it was lit only by the moon
and stars, and the hills sank inside
one another up every lane.
Was there ever a moon like this?
Above Dundonald the clouds part
and the night sky is what it was
at any time: too late to start
over, I picture that faint sheen
on fields, thick-set. They almost shine.

■

□

Most of the face is rubbed away
but you can tell it's smiling, though
some kind of blister or decay
has taken the mouth, and the eyes too:
in sunshine, with dark coming on
through from behind the bright-lit flesh
like slow mould over a damp-stain,
it's me grinning into the flash,
or at least you would imagine so;
and it's not a photograph, no.

□

■

The wallpaper that hugs my walls
with sun and sandcastles, toy trains,
changes itself when the night falls
and every lighter colour drains
away, so the repeating lines
of stylized birds, or clouds up high,
turn into cross faces, the signs
of trouble coming: I have to lie
through darkness and through that display
face-down, for I can't face away.

☐   ☐

■

The Atlantic, its excessive bright,
blotted out nearly everything
where sand-dunes and the hot sand let
me lounge for hours, as all along
that strand somewhere in Donegal
waves reared and thudded: pages were
so light they hurt, they were so full
of heat and sand, fetching from far
music, cyphers, monstrosities
reeling in black letters like these.

■   ☐

☐

□

My face was a three-year-old's, as
it sometimes is when I can't see
myself; then back just as it was –
no chin, pale-cheeked, old and jowly.
But once it was really a child's,
the smile ready and the eyes clear,
that face you saw: a crowd unfolds,
and lost children are everywhere
for seconds at a time, as they
work and weep, scramble, rush away.

□

■

□

Words going wrong, words going wrong
everywhere all the time; you catch
only the half of them, you bring
them down in heaps, you have to scratch
and scuttle through and scramble them
round and around and upside-down
until you give up, until from
the mess of letters that has grown
enormous not one word comes out
to comfort you by reading it.

■

■   □

He must have wanted a breath of air
after the whole day spent indoors,
for we've gone the length of Belvedere
Park, like a pair of wanderers
just starting out; but I'm the one
starting, taking him up the hill.
He can't see; and I'm seeing him
for the last time: there he is still,
tall, stooping, slow, helped all the way,
an old man being led by a boy.

Close up, very close, the finite
is everything, all poise and switch,
tilting itself into the light;
the insides of a pocket-watch
that still measures what the heart knows,
though it knows so little, and hangs on
to that while the dear life just goes
away on; the always foregone
conclusions of love; an opened door
at night-time: but the eye sees more.

I keep false-faces from Hallowe'en,
their cardboard sagging or plastic cracked,
in a shallow cupboard coming down
with precious junk I don't expect
to lose: the monster-mouths that gape,
and eyes that are just holes are there
at the back, starting to lose their shape,
perished and bent and broken – where
are they going to so gradually,
and what is left for them to see?

□■

■

□

Portstewart, on the low cliff-walk
one summer, and us on a bench
taking our ease; there was no talk,
and I was busy trying to scrunch
my eyes near-shut, so japs of light
could flicker up from the high tide,
each one a soul, a soul in flight –
I repeated that in my head
so preciously: I was fourteen
and didn't know, and you weren't gone.

□   □

■

Always a reader, she never read
again after her eyes went bad;
for weeks she did sums in her head,
not bothering to get out of bed:
never an idle day till then,
but then a gap, the time before
the end, everything uncertain
and the wrong thing – like the one hour
Lizzie burned her few photographs
with their unseeable joys and griefs.

Our churches smell, not of incense,
but of furniture-polish and fresh-
cut flowers: clear windows condense
the daylight as I watch it flash
from all the wood; I have to close
my eyes to pray, but this one day
they don't open again: suppose
I see Him in His house – glory
would dazzle me and blind me, so
I clench my eyelids, scared not to.

□

I have no need of eyes to see
again that plate of Blake's: an old
man stooping, leaning heavily
on a crutch as he nears the threshold.
His downward look speaks only of
the sadness in bending so low,
with each step weighted, to take leave:
there's nothing courtly in his bow
as he goes beneath the lintel of stone
from a dark place to a darker one.

■

□   □   ■

Too many   I won't go,
pretending not   them; look,
there they   and flow,
all at   □□   cracked Belleek
inside the bubble-wrap, now fixed
with glue – you'll never see the joins –
worthless old books with pages foxed,
bag after bag of copper coins
are, in their blur, places to see
once, jumbled, emblems of finity.

□□□□□

■

■   ■□

Not quite at once, but suddenly
enough daylight became a grid,
black and white squares all you could see
where half-shadows and outlines hid
themselves, came back or went away.
When I   □□□   ■■   phone ring,
        ■   □   ■   say
something to help, or anything
at all,   □   trace
    tear-tracks over your poor face.

■

Everything then a chequerboard,
criss-crossed, divided, cut in squares;
better, an unstarted crossword,
and in between its four corners
a random lattice for the light.
But it moved   □   □
it moved   lot
with it, until   ■■   went
receding ■□   each square
empty, as   □   never there.

■

first they sang
immutable
fountain   □   invisible
                    brightness where
throned ■   ■
         beams   through a cloud
    □□   like a radiant
dark   □   appear
yet dazzle   brightest
         □■□   wings veil

              ■

                something inside
        shadows breathing, or
                □   wears a hood
that it pulls back   □   floor
with wash on wash of dark
            ■   you to clean;
it keeps spilling, it keeps
                □□   where they've been.
But look, the   while you cry,
their wings   □   the shadows fly.

□□

            ■

        You wouldn't know him: did you know me
        the last time we met in that room?
        Only a voice edging softly
        out of the dark to say I'd come
        gave me away, and that voice was
        a face, though from goodness knows where:
        the wee boy who was at a loss
        when death came; beaten, and by then
        older than his years, in a sense
        gone like his features, gone long since?

                            □■

            ■

Your mother, busy all her life,
couldn't see to get out of bed
when the time came for you to leave;
your split lips, bruises on your head,
and your eye-sockets raw with tears
when Charlie came home and beat you
to keep you there – blind eyes like hers
were spared that, it was too late, too
much to see: far too much for you
to cover without it showing through.

□□

The day came when Bob Strickland could
see nothing but the Lord, and gave
all he owned, all he ever would,
to hands sure to redeem and save
poor sinners; as the poverty
got worse, he made out less and less
his wife, his daughters: one night, he
brought home a hatchet, went heedless
down the bright path that Jesus showed
him on the lower Braniel Road.

What happened to the colours? Black
and white: his pale skin and the thin
gray hair that's been combed flatly back,
the dark suit, the dark shirt, and then
dark glasses where his eyes should be,
the white dog-collar, the white stick,
are all I ever learn to see
in his crossing over and back
with God each summer from Stranraer,
not telling where the colours are.

□

■

I think now it was Narin strand;
the tide was covering our way
to Inishkeel; from end to end,
sunshine blowing the clouds away,
and that was the light I read in, read
the book you bought me, Yeats's plays,
cover to cover: where that led
was just Belfast, the boring days
on days of being – what, sixteen?
And no, you don't see what I mean.

■

It's dark before the pictures come:
happy in the News and Cartoon,
I'm waiting for their bright spectrum
as though I could touch it, breathe it in,
a colour-burst spinning across
from nowhere into College Square
to fill my eyes with light. The loss
is time's, but still five years before
that comes, and a bomb's handiwork
puts out the light, puts out the dark.

It moved after its light was spent,
unseeable then in the window
as though it might become fulgent
ever again, ever again; as though
we knew it once it was put out,
yet there was nothing that we knew.
You never had a minute's doubt,
did you? You saw it beaming through
where it had risen once and stood,
when it couldn't, and never could.

You have to bend down to get in,
and keep your head low, leaving all
the brightness you have ever seen
behind, and making yourself small
again, to fit the place for you
that can't be shown. And nothing next,
everywhere nothing: all the new
pages filling up with new text
have nothing in them, even if
you read them, or ever could have.

∎

□

I didn't know what I could say
to you after that night-terror
when he stood in his shadow: why
should he come back to loiter there
over your bedroom door, when he
was kind and careful to the last?
You saw his face: it was angry,
you said; and from then on, the best
thing was to keep the light on, or
maybe see nothing any more.

∎

Their arms are wings, and with those wings
they cover up their faces, veil
their eyes: the dazzling light belongs
elsewhere – something invisible
behind a full, excessive blaze
that means you cannot see. It's like
a language lost in its own ways,
abstractions with nowhere to look,
immutable great stones side-lit
and cold, immortal, infinite.

■

Once you died, I had nothing left
to give you: I took all you had,
leaving it out of reach in the loft
until the time I'm also dead.
I wrapped and boxed it, put it away:
maybe you're watching, maybe your
eyes pour out all the light of day
brighter than my own could endure;
the crystal animals in full blaze
with it; the china's flashing glaze.

■

This is me, wearing a false-face,
dawdling on the Gilnahirk Road
like the ghost who waited in that place
for Charlie one night; pay no heed
to shadows where my eyes should be,
or the slashed grin above my lips;
walk straight on past, and ignore me;
don't look at me if the mask slips
to show a freckled child's face there,
raw with need of you, shocked and bare.

■

Near the end of the very last
play, and fast running out of space,
when almost all that could be lost
is lost, he turns a covered face
away, and says that the blind know
everything; then the secret's out;
some birds wait for the light to go,
since there are no questions to put:
in the dark, you can hear them sing.
I think that you know everything.

■

□□□   □
            ■□■■

WOODSTOCK

The sun's angle is what makes me tall,
so my size is entirely accidental

as I pass Chaucer Cottage now, alone
(I think it was named after his son)

but going home; while darker than it all,
my own shadow is walking across the wall.

BREAKAGE

Not just the pieces smashed beneath
layers of padding, not just these,
or glass cracking to set your teeth
on edge: the minute things to seize

on are almost too small to see –
hairlines, but thinner than a hair,
that track themselves unfixably
where they had never been before,

or else flaws at the very start
building in weakness like a trap,
and fragile rhythms from the heart
abrupted by a dripping tap

to spoil that music. Nearly all
you love is broken, and can't last;
you'll live to see the value fall
as soon as tests stop being passed.

Only the perfect poems count;
only the paintings that are true:
when Rothko measured the amount
of dark, his black was deepest blue

and now, as you stand close to it,
it doesn't care, doesn't have to,
how much is broken, bit by bit,
ignoring and enclosing you.

FINIS AMORUM

At the end of the lane,
faint enough to be barely there
at all, faint and not moving, more than half
made out of light,

she is standing with a line
stretching towards and away from her,
a draughtsman's line, or a line on a graph,
to set me right –

for I might as well not
be here, and I am here too late:
age rots the spirit in its body-shell,
on its way where?

She marks the furthest spot
my eyes can reach, when absolute
blindness and dread take over for the kill;
dead in his armour,

the knight with a green plume
is going nowhere, pledged for good
to a name, to a few words, to his own end:
and now she brings

angled, retreating flame
to stone, steel, the path where he stood;
to everywhere: the last light she can lend
these smallest things.

THE STORK

Fifty years and more it had
balanced on one leg
there in the china-cabinet,
plucked from a christening cake

beside two napkin-rings, and a
silver spoon with my name;
hard icing, and an icing beak
that held in its own napkin

what was meant for a baby: it
was where I came from.
Drier for the years, more brittle,
the figure never broke,

but today as I set about
a dust-down and a clear-out
of that final sitting-room,
my hand where it reached back

touched what felt like glue,
and I looked and I saw the stork,
its head dropped, swollen, embryo-
heavy, with one eye cocked

at me, and its leg buckled,
the bundle it had carried once
no more than a slick trickle,
what was left of endurance;

then I scooped it up in paper, and
threw the paper away; I wiped
where it had been melted and unstuck,
to make its end a clean end.

WEAVELEY FURZE (2)

for S.R.

Maytime now, and the butterflies are
starting to be everywhere, all across
this path between fields of rape;
although you are really no more here
than he was, walk alongside me, as
I try my hardest to play catch-up
with their paper-light, freed colours
that begin and stop

spiriting themselves through the morning sun:
I think you're still able to look askance
at me when I intone
(*basso profundo*) that line – *unawares
morality expires*; and lower still, *Yes,
Yes* – the sad little monkey-man,
derided, lethal, wrote it once,
and he's long gone,

though the butterflies, with much still to do,
manage to stick around: for a second, I'm struck
with how they fly staying low,
and how quickly they move forward and back,
like this one with the cream-white wings, dipped
in *Kia-Ora* orange – that exactly –
who in only a moment has slipped
entirely away from me

and out across the big field, to a corner
of stalks and yellow blooms. The souls, *caro*,
the souls we loved are tiny and
bright and everywhere; *the living God*, though,
imagine that: is it really so fearful
to fall into those hands, when no
sooner have we fallen than
– look – he lets us go?

2018

NOTES AND ACKNOWLEDGEMENTS

Epigraphs
Geoffrey Chaucer, *The Merchant's Tale*, 69-70.
Emily Dickinson, poem 258 ('There's a certain Slant of light'), 14.

The drovers' road
Epigraph from W.B. Yeats, 'The Happy Townland', 47-48.

Success
After Pindar, *Isthmian* 5, 12-16.

At Newcastle Island
Newcastle Island is near Nanaimo, British Columbia.

To fall into the hands
Hebrews 10.31: 'It is a fearful thing to fall into the hands of the living God'.

Mud
Epigraph from Geoffrey Hill, *Scenes from Comus* (2005), 'Courtly Masquing Dances: *nello stile antico*', 67.
1. '*wrote by saving himself from the mud | of Flanders*': Stephen Spender, 'Tragedy and Some Modern Poetry', *Penguin New Writing* 4 (March 1941), 147:

> Yeats wrote by saving himself from the mud of Flanders and the mud of the common mind of his time. He is an isolated figure who achieved greatness. Other poets may admire him, but they cannot follow him, because he does not wrestle with the problem

of interpreting the surrounding life of his time into poetry. He is only himself.

4. E.R. Dodds (1893–1979) was Regius Professor of Greek in the University of Oxford 1936-1960. J.D. Denniston (1887–1949) and Maurice Bowra (1898–1971) had both anticipated taking the Regius Chair in 1936; it was given to Dodds on the recommendation to Downing Street of Gilbert Murray (1866–1957), who had held it himself since 1908. See E.R. Dodds, *Missing Persons* (1977).

Sooth
the sooth voice of the shade: John Keats, 'The Fall of Hyperion: A Dream' (1819), I, 155.

The other side
The panel by Filippino Lippi, *The Wounded Centaur* (Christ Church Picture Gallery, Oxford) has on its reverse an unfinished work, variously identified as a *Triumph of Love* or *Allegory of Fortune*, by the same artist.

The party
After Horace, *Odes* 4.11.

Guinea
Epigraph: William Blake, *Visions of the Daughters of Albion* (1793), Plate 1.

Blindness
Several sections of this poem quote from or allude to John Milton, *Paradise Lost* (1667), III, 372-382:

Thee Father first they sung Omnipotent,
Immutable, Immortal, Infinite,
Eternal King; thee Author of all being,
Fountain of Light, thy self invisible

Amidst the glorious brightness where thou sit'st
Thron'd inaccessible, but when thou shad'st
The full blaze of thy beams, and through a cloud
Drawn round about thee like a radiant Shrine,
Dark with excessive bright thy skirts appeer,
Yet dazle Heav'n, that brightest Seraphim
Approach not, but with both wings veil thir eyes.

Weaveley Furze (2)
unawares morality expires: Alexander Pope, *The Dunciad* (1743), IV, 649-650: '*Religion* blushing veils her sacred fires, | And unawares *Morality* expires'.

*

The author is grateful to the editors of the following publications, in which some of these poems first appeared: *Agenda, Literary Imagination, Literary Matters*.

'The Other Side' was published as a limited edition in the *Tower Gallery Poems* series by Tower Poetry, Christ Church (2017).

It's as well   you knew is gone
                not to know all
the senses first   even a thing
                sense isn't
places gone   one by one
                somewhere times
so what   to say alone
                could it ever mean
and sleeping like   oh like a doll
                 a doll

                                      sleeping